STRESS – THE REALITY

The Practical 'How To' Guide on Achieving Less Stress in Your Life.

+50 Top Tips for Solving Stress

JULIE HOGBIN

Conscious Leadership for Business & Life

On Point Series – by Julie Hogbin

1. Setting Goals. Life and Business Changing Magic. How to set Goals Inspiring and Sustaining Action.
2. STRESS – The Reality. The Practical 'How To' Guide on Achieving Less Stress in Your Life. + 50 Top Tips for Solving Stress

ISBN: 9798645659929

Published June 2020 - London UK
Business Talks and Workshops

www.JulieHogbin.com
www.CLAVEM.global

Contents

Please connect with me on all the normal social media platforms

Please connect on:
Linkedin Julie Hogbin
Facebook Page Julie Hogbin CLAVEM
Facebook Group Conscious Leadership CLAVEM
Instagram Julie Hogbin
Podcast Conscious Leadership on all platforms
YouTube Conscious Leadership

 The Key To success

Stress – The Reality

Julie Hogbin

Dedication

I dedicate this book to all of those that have experienced Stress and to all of you who have spoken to me about it.

Without you this book would not have been written, for you have provided me with experiences, creating the passion, for preventative, proactive stress management.

I also dedicate it to all of you who apply the learnings from this book to prevent you from experiencing the decimating circumstances of stress.

For all our conversations and trust

I thank you

Julia

Stress – The Reality

Acknowledgements

A special thanks to Ruth Sullivan for her support and generosity not only to me but also to her Rising Tide group.

Thank you, Ruth, without you this would not have happened, well certainly not now. The timing was right the synchronicity was magical and your expertise a fathomless depth.

www.RuthESullivan.com

Stress – The Reality

Introduction

I have spent the last 30+ years working within the learning and development field within business and life as a coach, mentor, and trainer.

I have worked alongside 10s of thousands of individuals and I have come across many who are stressed, both young and old, at the beginning and end of their career, across genders and disciplines.

I have come to the understanding that stress can destroy individuals and businesses and negatively affect people for a long time, both those experiencing it and those around them! I do not need to be a medically trained individual to know and understand that.

However, what I do know is that we can proactively manage our stress levels so that we do not end up in a bad place. Now I have experienced stress without knowing or understanding what it was and not knowing or understanding how I could have done anything differently. How can you when you don't know anything about the subject?

Recognising that pressure accrues to create stress from both a positive, eustress, and negative start, distress, was an absolute eye-opener for me.

That knowledge set me on a mission to share the information I have amassed over decades, to support others to live their lives well.

I am now aware of the importance of recognising stress in advance, so that the warning signals may be picked up in time and a course of action implemented before any illness is realised.

► We have choices in how we respond,
► We have choices in how we allow the triggers to affect us.
► We have choices in what organisation and manager we work for.
► We have choices in our life partners and family.
► We have choices in how we fuel our bodies.

We have so many choices that sometimes we don't believe we can choose! and we choose, instead, to make ourselves victims.

Some of those choices will be harder to implement than others and if we are making the choices with the right information for the right reasons, they are always easier to make and there is always a difference between making the choice and taking the action.

> *'To know is to grow and for us to grow, action is required'*
>
> *Julie Hogbin*

I anticipate this book will give you valuable information to enable you in making more informed choices, choices which empower you, your life, your business, and for those around you.

This applies whether you are employed, self-employed, a business owner, an entrepreneur, a chief executive, or somebody starting on their career journey.

It is relevant to everyone whether you are a mother, father, daughter, a sister, an aunt, an uncle, a son or brother, or, indeed, anyone else that I may have missed on that list

Stress
Does not go hand-in-hand with success; it
Does not go hand-in-hand with a position; in fact, it
Does not go hand-in-hand with life. Full stop!

When you are stressed, there is a tendency for you to become something other than you truly are; your reactions are different, your results are different, your decisions are made with and from a stressed thought process.

This book is full of practical advice and some of the technical jargon that will help you to understand the effects of too much pressure on your body and how it changes your functioning system

This book is for anyone, regardless of who you are, to gain the knowledge and practical advice to live a stress-free life wherever you are in the world.

The Dalai Lama when asked what surprised him most about humanity said:

"Man because he sacrifices his health in order to make money, then he sacrifices money to recuperate his health, and then he is so anxious about the future that he does not enjoy the present.

The result being that he does not live in the present or the future,

he lives as if he is never going to die and then dies having never really lived."

Chapter 1 - Context What is Stress and What Does it Cost?

Definition – What is Stress?

Stress is people's natural reaction to excessive pressure; it is not a disease or something you catch.

Stress is when we as the individual cannot cope with the additional demand of an additional pressure being put upon us and it tips us over the edge. We stoop, we trip, we stumble, then we fall. When we are managing well, our coping strategies are working well, and we can balance the demands made upon us, we can put ourselves back into a balanced position, we stand upright and walk tall.

When we cannot cope with the additional pressure and we cannot rebalance is when we can legitimately say we are experiencing stress – it is the proverbial straw that broke the camel's back and a straw is very light – it is just the final thing that tips us over the edge. In my case it was driving a new car (and I love cars & driving)

Stress is one of those words that is banded about when we generally mean we are under pressure and it has become common parlance without the word being truly understood.

I will always look at the origins of any word and stress which originates from Latin is *'strictus'* which means 'drawn tight' and that is exactly what it can feel like.

We can stress test something to push it to a breaking point and that, of course, is NOT what we need to be doing with our human body.

"an engineers viewpoint! If you occasionally run an engine above the 'red line', it will probably complete its journey, as long, as it is routinely serviced. If you run it consistently above the 'red line' it will certainly fail but you won't know when; until it happens."

It is the same with us as humans, we may think all is well and then one day it just isn't anymore, and something gives and our engine blows.

Regular servicing is required for us, our body and our mind, our health as well. We have an engine, a chassis, an exhaust in one way or another. Remaining healthy is the similar for us as it is a car!

A true story: *A young retail store manager who was running a successful branch on The Wirral told me a story of himself.*

He was about 25 when it happened and told me his story roughly 10 years later when he felt able to share.

He was doing well with his work, he was getting great results, he enjoyed his job and the people he worked with.

He had a young family and partner who he loved, his Nan had died, and his father had health issues and he was supporting his Mother and Father.

He remembers locking the shop up and leaving to walk home. 10 days later he woke up in the hospital!

He literally broke and had no idea what happened or why. He was told he was stressed, he perceived it as an unknown weakness and a failure until he attended my course. He didn't share and he didn't talk about it, perceiving it as a weakness.

He then worked out what had happened. He had ignored any signs as he had no idea what they meant – nobody knows what they do not know.

It took him years to get his health back and he was understandably careful with it.

An excess of pressure that you, as the individual you are, do not have the capabilities to deal with can lead to stress and, if stress is excessive and goes on for some time, it can lead to both mental and physical health deterioration.

Is stress a good thing? No, not at all, unless it is saving our life. Being under pressure often improves performance and pressure is a good thing but, when demands and pressures become unbalanced linked to our ability to deal with them, it can lead to stress, stress, and the symptoms that are caused are bad for you.

Costs of Stress – Business

Work-related stress, depression or anxiety continues to represent a significant ill health condition in the workforce of Great Britain (where I am based) It accounted for 44% of work-related ill health and 54% of working days lost, in 2018/19.

Poor productivity and days off sick are costing the UK, and globally, a staggering amount of money; sickness-related absences and presenteeism are costing the UK economy £77.5 billion a year.

BUT It isn't about work as such, it is about us and the life we lead or is life leading us?

The occupations and industries reporting the highest rates of work-related stress, depression, or anxiety remain consistently in the health and public sectors of the economy and the highest percentage is from the professional roles within those sectors.

The reasons cited as causes of work-related stress are also consistent over time with workload, lack of managerial support and organisational change as the primary causative factors.

These figures are from organisations that report not from everyday life or those that do not speak up.

Cost of Stress – Personal

How can we define the cost of stress to us personally? Either short or long term.

What price can we put on the damage to our health, to our relationships, to our families, to our career, to our success and over how many years?

The cost is an insurmountable figure to calculate, it certainly is not an equation we can work with as a whole as we are all so different.

Age and Gender

From the research conducted throughout 2018/2019 **females** had statistically significantly higher rates of work-related stress, depression, and anxiety compared with the average for all persons, male and female. The research was conducted within the age range of 16 – 55+ with the age ranges most affected being 25 – 54

Absenteeism

There were 12.8 million days lost in total which, on average, equates to 21.2 days lost from work per case and the number of new incidences was 246,000, 740 per 100,000. It is estimated that £42.6 billion is lost through absenteeism

Presenteeism

It is estimated that £34.9 billion is lost through presenteeism, which is defined as: *reduced productivity among people who are at work but unwell.*

This means that mental health problems cost £1,300 for every employee in the UK economy. Another estimate indicates that one in five working people will have a mental health difficulty and many will never get any help – this is unacceptable and we need to do something about it.

Chapter 2 – The Technical 'stuff'

How does stress happen? This is one of my favourite understandings, how the body works, and how it changes from when we are normal (whatever that means) to when we are stressed.

In this wonderful 21st Century, we have improved our intelligence levels, we know more, the technology we use has improved, we can get places faster than we ever have done before, we can communicate globally with ease and work from many, many places. We have electricity and cars that run on electricity, we have satellites and systems that provide us with the WWW and Wi-Fi and we have global news at the touch of the button 24/7 and medical facilities that can replace hearts and joints!

In reality, our body and how it operates is the same as it has always been from our Neanderthal roots – nothing has changed.

Neanderthal mans cycle of response to pressure

What Stress Does to Us

We are a bundle of nerves and we have billions of interconnecting nerve cells that allow the body to function. Every cell in the human body is influenced in one way or another by the nervous system. The nervous system is our onboard computer with its own memory drive which runs on a highly sophisticated software

We feed information into that system through our sense organs which are then modified by higher mental functions in the brain, which produce reactions and instructions transmitted along nerve cells to the rest of the body

Stressful stimuli affect our nervous system which, in turn, acts in a way that is guaranteed to make us respond.

This was one of my eye-opening moments when I realised how the biology of the body concerning a stress response could change how our body functions and the effect that can have on our health and personality.

Please remember that every one of us is different, in accordance with our coping capability. Which will come from our upbringing, our culture, our environment, our education, our personality type,

and all of the life experiences we have accrued from wherever we have accrued them.
All of these will help us respond and get ourselves back into balance when the body shifts us to a stress response to a situation.

Our stress response is commonly called 'fight or flight' and that is exactly what our body prepares us to do still to this day! We think we can control it and we can't.

Fight, Flight or Freeze

The nervous system has many functions, some are controllable, and some are performed automatically, the most basic and primitive function of all is that of survival itself.

A personal story:
A friend of mine once chain-sawed his leg and walked half a mile to get to a phone and there wasn't a drop of blood to be seen - his survival instinct kicked in and knowing that blood loss would weaken him his body restricted that happening.

Now I mention this because I physically saw no blood and was with him until the ambulance arrived.

There are many stories of people completing magnificent feats of endurance and survival in extreme circumstances.

The survival response prepares us within milliseconds to meet any life-threatening event head on - our flight or fight reaction has remained unchanged since time immemorial.

In Neanderthal man, the fight or flight reaction prepared him for the ultimate physical challenge. He would either stand and fight the wild animal or foe or run to safety as fast as he possibly could. If he froze, he would very possibly die. It was a far rawer society back then than now.

The fight or flight reaction is a lifesaver and is every bit as appropriate and vital now as it was then.

This would be called an acute response and we have no control over it, our body does it for us automatically.

How Does Stress Work?

A complex series of biological changes occur automatically, in the basic format your body is preparing itself to run or fight.

The heart will beat faster and blood pressure will rise, breathing will quicken and reflexes sharpen, muscles will fill with blood and skin will cool and sweat, extra glucose would pump into the bloodstream and mental alertness will be heightened and focused.

Fighting ability will be enhanced to a degree that would be impossible during any moment of relaxation. There will be extra oxygen in the lungs and circulation increases pumping blood to the muscles enabling you to run more swiftly than any other time.

A personal story:

When I was a young girl, a friend and I ended up locked in a garage of an older boy with the threat that he would hurt us if we moved!

Now I know now that my survival instinct is strong and as a young child, all I knew that all I had to do was get out of there, which my friend and I did.

The interesting part of all this concerning our automatic responses is that my friend was the County champion for the 100-metre sprint, and I beat her to get away - I never managed that speed again.

Was I in greater acute stress response than her?

Who knows, but I do recall that, at the time I felt my life was in danger.

The fight or flight response is created to save our life from a threat. What our body doesn't know is the difference between real or perceived threat. Our body has two states to be in; aroused or relaxed. When it is aroused, it is fight-flight functioning and when it is relaxed it is in safe mode.

We all go through life responding to the pressures around us; we first become mentally aroused to meet the challenge and then relax as each crisis passes

Whether we are aroused or relaxed depends entirely on the nervous system which has two independent branches working in opposition to one another. These are the sympathetic branch (aroused) and the parasympathetic branch (relaxed).

The carefully orchestrated yet near-instantaneous sequence of hormonal changes and physiological responses helps someone to fight the threat off or flee to safety.

So what triggers the response in the first place? It is our perception of danger, pure and simple. Each one of us knows that if we see a rampant bull elephant charging us or a pack of lions hunting us, we know it is a life-threatening moment.

If we are faced with a knife-wielding maniac, a car heading directly towards us, we know it is a life-threatening moment and we do something.

But what about if you are stuck in a traffic jam, about to go on stage and speak to an audience of 2,000, need to have a conversation with a senior manager about a situation or you are about to sit an exam?

Are the second situations life-threatening? "No" is the answer in reality, but if we perceive them to be, our body reacts as though we are in a life or death situation.

Unfortunately, the body can also overreact to stressors that are not life-threatening, these minor irritations and frustrations which accumulate in number and which are repeated regularly, can trigger a different but significant stress response.

This type of stress response is less powerful than the flight or fight reaction and considerably more sinister.

It produces many of the same effects but to a much lesser degree and the person affected is consequently much less aware of the effects on their emotions and their body

Over time, repeated activation or continuance of the stress response takes an incredible toll on our body, especially when we are aroused without reclaiming the relaxed condition.

None of us are exempt from the stress response

The Command Centre

We take in information through our senses; sight, smell, hearing, touch & taste, and each one of those can trigger the stress response within us.

We are all individuals in our own right and what may trigger the stress response in one will not trigger it in another.

What one person can deal with and relish, another will fear.

Sounding the Alarm

The stress response begins in the brain (cerebral cortex). When someone confronts a perceived danger, real as in a speeding car, or imagined their senses, one or a few combined, send the information to the amygdala, which is the area of the brain that contributes to emotional processing. The amygdala interprets the images and sounds and when it perceives danger, it instantly sends a distress signal to the hypothalamus which then changes how the body functions.

The hypothalamus sends its messages into our system and changes the purpose of our system.

The Technical Bit

The **cerebral cortex** is responsible for many higher-order brain functions such as sensation, perception, memory, association, thought, and voluntary physical activity. The cerebrum is the large, main part of the brain and serves as the thought and control centre.

The **amygdala** is an area of the brain that contributes to emotional processing; it sends a distress signal to the hypothalamus.

The **hypothalamus** is the part of the brain that maintains the body's internal balance. The hypothalamus produces releasing and inhibiting hormones, which stop and start the production of other hormones throughout the body.

This area of the brain functions like a command centre, communicating with the rest of the body through the nervous system so that the person has the energy to fight or flee.

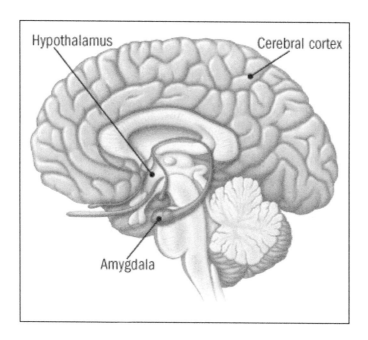

The **autonomic nervous system** is the part of the **nervous system** that supplies the internal organs, including the blood vessels, stomach, intestine, liver, kidneys, bladder, genitals, lungs, pupils, heart, and sweat, salivary, and digestive glands, and it has two main divisions which work in opposition to each other.

Sympathetic – Aroused - Parasympathetic - Relaxed

Sympathetic Arousal	GENERALLY	Parasympathetic Relaxed
Fight & Flight	GENERALLY	At rest
Alert (initially)	BRAIN	Calm
Pupils widen	EYES	Constricted
Drys	SALIVA	Normal
Widen	AIRWAYS	Normal
Fast	HEART	Normal
Thickens	BLOOD	Flows easily
Widens in	BLOOD VESSELS	Widens in
the heart & limb		the skin
Tense	MUSCLES	Relaxed
Decreased	INTESTINE	Increased
Inhibited	GUT	Normal
Utilises stored red blood cells	SPLEEN	Fights Bacteria
Inhibits Voiding	BOWEL	Normal
Increases to the skin	SWEATING	Normal
Glucose production & released into circulation	LIVER	Normal

JulieHogbin©

The Long-Term Effects of Stress

Over time, repeated activation of the stress response takes a toll on the body slowly and surely, and if we never manage to get the body back to a relaxed state, the body is silently damaged.

Unless we are conscious of what is going on for us, stress will build up over time and can have serious consequences for both our physical and mental health. I include emotional health within the mental sphere.

So Why and How Does This Happen?

Modern-day society is so very different from how our Neanderthal ancestors lived, and how our body still naturally operates. If we reacted now in the same way as they used to, we would probably all be incarcerated by now! Or we would spend our life running away and starting afresh. Which some still do as do some still fight.

In reality, what happens is that we do not fight, and we do not run; it is not socially acceptable.

Therefore, we stay in the situation and continue to experience the 'thing' that is upsetting us.

There is a tendency to be more concerned about what others may think about us and our behaviours than is healthy for us. It is natural for us to want to be liked, to fit in, and to be part of a community, and it is that desire to be accepted which can lead us to not recognising how that may be affecting us.

Sympathetic Arousal – fight & flight

	Short Term	Long Term
Brain	Faster functioning, better memory & concentration	Headaches, migraine, overwhelm, confusion, cloudy thought, depression
Eyes	See everything, periphery alert	Tired, blurry, itchy, dry
Saliva	Dry	Very dry & dehydrated
Heart	Faster pulse & higher blood pressure to assist	High pressure, chest pain, working harder
Bood	Is thicker	Sticky and slow moving
Muscles	Alert, faster, powerful	Tension, Pain
Intestine	Slow digestion, blood supply reduced	Ulcers, IBS, heartburn, indigestion, bloating
Bladder	Urinate regularly	Discomfort
Skin	Cool & Sweaty	Blemishes, spots, eczema, rashes
Lungs	Oxygen sent to bloodstream	Breathlessness, asthma, feeling of suffocation
Sexual	Impotence in men, disturbed menstrual cycle in women	Loss of sexual drive and interest

Chapter 3
Self-Assessment and Prediction

The Most Common Sources of Stress

Please remember that pressure is applied from positive action, eustress, as well as negative, distress; any level of additional pressure is fine if our coping strategies and abilities are capable to deal with it.

There is the concept of eustress which produces positive feelings of excitement, fulfilment, meaning, satisfaction, and well-being, which leads to feelings of confidence as you are stimulated from the challenge the stressor applies.

There is the concept of distress which produces negative feelings of extreme sorrow, anxiety, pain, or fear. Which can lead to loss of self-esteem and confidence.

When either of these additional pressures are prolonged, intense, and combined, no matter how well equipped we are to deal with them, or how much we enjoy them, we will ultimately break.

It is the combination that accrues the points and the power over the body.

One of the best-known questionnaires to support us in this prediction is the Holmes-Rahe Social Readjustment Rating Scale which I have replicated here.

We can assess the likelihood of us experiencing stress by adding up points allocated to each incidence that has happened to us during the last 12 months.

The questionnaire is broken down into family, personal, work, and financial areas. The researchers initially questioned several hundred people about their circumstances which had necessitated the most 'social readjustment' and which were frequently stressful.

An arbitrary value of 100 life change units was given to the death of a partner and all other sources of stress were measured to this.

Holmes-Rahe Social Readjustment Rating Scale

Please ring the events, from the following 43, that you have experienced in the last 12 months and total the points

	Life Event	Mean Value
1	Death of spouse - partner	100
2	Divorce	73
3	Marital separation from partner	65
4	Detention in jail or other institution	63

5	Death of a close family member	63
6	Major personal injury or illness	53
7	Marriage	50
8	Being fired at work or redundancy	47
9	Marital reconciliation with partner	45
10	Retirement from work	45
11	A major change in the health or behaviour of a family member	44
12	Pregnancy	40
13	Sexual difficulties	39
14	Gaining a new family member - birth, adoption, older or younger adult moving in	39
15	Major business readjustment	39
16	Major change in financial state - worse or better off than usual	38
17	Death of a close friend	37
18	Changing to a different line of work	36
19	A major change in the number of arguments with a partner - either a lot more or a lot less than usual to include child-rearing, personal habits, etc	35
20	Taking on a mortgage for home or business	31
21	Foreclosure/repossession on a mortgage or loan	30
22	Major change in responsibilities at work - promotion, demotion, acting up	29
23	Son or daughter leaving home - marriage, leaving home, college, etc	29
24	In-law troubles	29
25	Outstanding personal achievement	28
26	Spouse /partner beginning or ceasing work outside of the home	26
27	Beginning or ceasing formal education	26
28	Major change in living condition - new home, remodelling, deterioration of neighbourhood or home	25
29	Revision of personal habits - dress, manners, associations, quitting smoking	24
30	Troubles with the boss	23
31	Major changes in working hours or conditions	20
32	Changes in residence	20
33	Changing to a new school	20

34	Major change in usual type or amount of recreation	19
35	Major change in church activity - a lot more or a lot less	19
36	Major change in social activities - clubs, movies, visiting etc	18
37	Taking on a loan - car, TV etc	17
38	Major change in sleeping habits - a lot more or a lot less than usual	16
39	A major change in the number of family get-togethers	15
40	Major change in eating habits - a lot more or less food intake or different meal hours or surroundings	15
41	Vacation - Christmas coming soon	13
42	Major Holidays	12
43	Minor violations of the law - traffic tickets, disturbing the peace, etc	11
	TOTAL	

It is estimated that any score 150 - 300 is associated with a 50% chance of a health breakdown in the next 2 years

A score of over 300 is associated with an 80% chance during the following two years

It is the lucky few who have a score of less than 150, indicating a low amount of life change, who are considered to have no increased health risk.

NOTE: This scale is not a predictor of illness. It merely indicates that there may be an increased risk to you, by being aware and managing yourself the risk can be reduced.

REMEMBER stress is unresolved pressure

It seems an appropriate point to mention my story and what happened to me.

> **A personal story:**
> I was around 28 at the time and had been married for four years and I already knew that the marriage was not successful. My partner and I were arguing, and he had said he didn't want children as he was feeling trapped enough by the marriage, let alone having screaming kids around him!
>
> Now, with the benefit of hindsight, that was a defining moment in my life, and without that, I certainly would not be where I am today.
>
> Along with that, one Saturday morning he accused me of trying to poison him!! All I was doing was cleaning his flask out. This was the straw that broke the camels back on the marriage.
>
> The marriage ended. I moved back home to my parents, and a long, drawn-out divorce started. It took nearly 2 years. We had two cars at the time, and I took the one with the least value, I woke up one morning and he had 'reclaimed' it shall I say!

At the same time as all this was happening, I changed jobs and started a new relationship. The new relationship introduced me to new people, new experiences, and a new life which was fun, lively, and a whole new world to me. It was fabulous and It was not just a fleeting relationship it lasted for 12 years.

18 months into the new relationship one Sunday lunch my partner offered me the opportunity to drive his brand-new Range Rover to the pub, which I did with glee (I love cars). I truly didn't know that that would be the straw that broke the camel's back!

I was fit, I was healthy, I was enjoying life and yet that Sunday lunchtime I could not physically pick up a drink from the bar, as my arms were shaking so much.

Although nothing unusual happened on that drive, that small amount of additional pressure applied to the amount I was already carrying, tipped me over the edge.

I had no idea what was going on and drank that first drink through a straw (there is an irony in that!)

Whatever happened became an ongoing condition for me to deal with which I did by utilising strategies that prevented me from having to pick up a glass, a

Hormonal Change

The adrenal glands, which are situated above each kidney, play a major part in the stress response; they produce three hormones whenever the body is under stress:
1. Adrenaline
2. Noradrenalin
3. Cortisol

Cortisol

Cortisol is the body's anti-inflammatory hormone - It fights inflammation, disease, and infection. It mops up and deals with cells that are not healthy and eradicates them and it can only do this when it is in relaxed mode.

It assists the other stress hormones to do their job efficiently and also helps to breakdown the body's fat stores and turn them into a source of energy for the muscles – it changes its job!

Cortisol can alter or shut down functions that get in the way. These might include your digestive or reproductive systems, your immune system, or even your growth processes.

Think of Cortisol as nature's built-in alarm system. It's your body's main stress hormone. It works with certain parts of your brain to control your mood, motivation, and fear.

It is your Adrenal glands that produce Cortisol which is best known for helping fuel your body's "fight-or-flight" instinct in a crisis

In a relaxed body, it plays an important role in several things your body does.

For example, it:
► Manages how your body uses carbohydrates, fats, and proteins
► Keeps inflammation down
► Regulates your blood pressure
► Increases your blood sugar (glucose)
► Controls your sleep/wake cycle
► Eradicates unhealthy cells
► Boosts energy so you can handle stress and restores balance afterwards

Acute stress is brought about by the effect of Noradrenaline and Adrenaline and only lasts for a few seconds. Hormones released into the circulation by the adrenal glands circulate much more slowly to the body's organs, therefore, the effect is delayed but once circulating these hormones maintain and prolong the stress response.

Because Cortisol has two separate mechanisms, the body can sustain the stress response for as long as is necessary to successfully deal with any challenging situation.

When the source of stress is abolished, the arousal, state is switched off and the relaxed state takes us back to normal operating procedure.

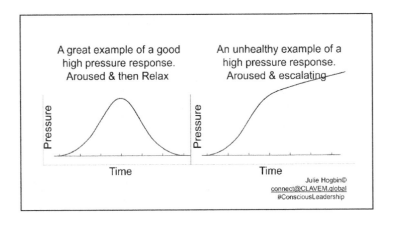

Adrenaline & Noradrenaline

While adrenalin has slightly more of an effect on your heart, noradrenaline has more of an effect on your blood vessels.

Between them they Increase the blood flow to muscles, increase the output of the heart, increase blood pressure, widening of airways, create pupil dilation, increase the blood sugar level, and narrowing of blood vessels in non-essential organs.

All in preparation for Fight or Flight

Stress-Induced Conditions

Some medical conditions that are now widely recognised as being induced by stress.

- ► Heart attack & Angina
- ► Diabetes
- ► Stroke
- ► Migraine
- ► Ulcers
- ► Asthma
- ► Depression
- ► Anxiety
- ► Obesity
- ► Anorexia
- ► Insomnia
- ► High blood pressure
- ► Sterility & Impotence
- ► IBS (Irritable Bowel syndrome)
- ► Adrenal fatigue
- ► Cancer

The above is not a comprehensive list and of course, they are not always induced by stress.

What it does mean is that they may be, and it is worth reflecting on what is happening for you.

Looking at the list how many are you experiencing and start to think about how long you may have been experiencing them and what you can do about them?

If you are experiencing a breakout of spots it may just be due to overindulging in chocolate and my question would be: What created the need to eat so much chocolate?

If you are experiencing muscle tension look at your lifestyle and assess what you can do to change it.

Tracking the symptom back to the root cause there will be something to work with and I expect that, when addressed, will put you into a relaxed state more frequently.

What do you think?

Chapter 5
How Does our Personality Affect our Stress?

We differ dramatically in our response to a problem or a stressor. Some of us are born with or create an operating system that influences us to higher or lower levels of tolerance to stress and stressors.

Your thoughts, and how you think and react to a situation play a role in determining how stressful a situation is to you – that sort of goes without saying and it needs to be written to be read.

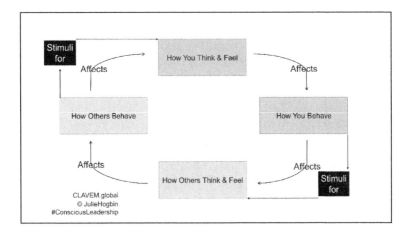

Many situations that lead to stress will have another individual, or group involved in the situation.

We can develop situational responses, and many of our stress reactions will be in how we perceive the situations around us.

> *'The more we can learn to respond rather than react to a situation the better equipped we will be both short and long term.'*
>
> *Julie Hogbin*

Type A & B Personalities

In the 1950s research completed by 2 cardiologists, Mayer Friedman and Ray Rosenman observed a relationship between incidences of heart disease and personality type and the term personality A was coined along with personality B.

Type A and B are basically the opposite of each other and as much as type C and type D have appeared since, and there are many other personality type profiles and questionnaires in existence now, I am a licenced practitioner of a select few, this basic A and B concept is a great learning tool especially linked to stress.

This original research provides us with an easy and very quick assessment of our primary tendency and how that would relate to our tendencies with creating stress for ourselves.

As a note, the findings were conducted over eight years and 1,500 individuals.

It is my personal belief that some of the best research for all sorts of theoretical information was completed in the 1950s and still stands in the 21st Century. Remembering of course that our bodies reaction has not changed for millenniums!

Type A Is described as people who want to get a lot of things completed and get irritated if their goals or their progress towards their goal is blocked. Type A gets frustrated by anything that slows their progress, wasting time, and stops them from getting things done.

Type A are naturally fidgety and impatient and characteristically are unable to sit still for more than a few minutes, they have self-imposed deadlines and may have been described as a perfectionist, an overachiever, and sometimes even a workaholic. This can lead to people not being able to keep up with a type-A personality either in conversation or movement, they are quick and want a result.

They are driven and focused on the goal and can tend to be less accepting of others who do not keep up.

Type A personality tend to also put their career and results above relationships and family.

Basically, with type A everything is urgent, now we may not know that as they tend to not express what is going on for them.

They may just scream silently and loudly in their own head

Type B personalities are easy going calm and controlled, content with their lives and are not easily upset or irritated.

This does not mean that they are not ambitious nor competitive they just have a different way of going about it.

One of the main differences between type A and type B is that type B can achieve the same result as type A and not make themselves ill in the process

Now, of course, we will never be entirely type A or type B we have a mixture of both at different times, in different circumstances, and different situations.

We are all on the spectrum with type A at one end and type B at the other in their extreme formats.

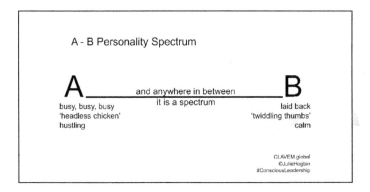

Where we sit on the spectrum depends on how we operate and function. We, of course, have choices to make on how we think, feel, and behave.

The choices we have are present for us all of the time, and unless we raise our self-awareness, we will continue doing the same thing over and over.

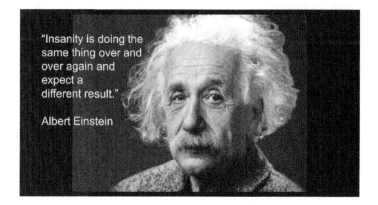

"Insanity is doing the same thing over and over again and expect a different result."

Albert Einstein

Julie Hogbin

Self-Assessment

Self-assessment increases self-awareness and with increased self-awareness, we can make choices consciously to do something different.

When we do something differently, we achieve a different result.

As they say, practice makes perfect and of course, practice also makes permanent.

The maximum score on the questionnaire is 120 and the lowest would be 12. There is, in reality, no scientific research to this questionnaire or the result.

The questions I have asked are linked to the main areas that a type A personality would score highly on and the type A personality is the one who is more prone to experience stress and the related illnesses that are associated.

I have answered this questionnaire a few times over the years and I have type A personality traits! When I received 9 speeding points on my driving license, 6 in one go, I truly learned how to 'adjust' my thoughts and behaviours.

Stress – The Reality

Please complete the following questionnaire to find out where your tendencies fall.

1	Do you find yourself in a hurry more often than not?
	Yes 10 9 8 7 6 5 4 3 2 1 No
2	Do you find it annoying and frustrating to queue or sit in traffic?
	Yes 10 9 8 7 6 5 4 3 2 1 No
3	Do you need to be in control?
	Yes 10 9 8 7 6 5 4 3 2 1 No
4	Do you do things at speed eating, talking, walking, driving?
	Yes 10 9 8 7 6 5 4 3 2 1 No
5	Are you more competitive than most?
	Yes 10 9 8 7 6 5 4 3 2 1 No
6	Do you do more than one thing at a time? Listen to a podcast, sort papers, make a call, read messages
	Yes 10 9 8 7 6 5 4 3 2 1 No
7	Would you consider yourself ambitious?
	Yes 10 9 8 7 6 5 4 3 2 1 No
8	Are you irritated by people who do not get to the point quickly?
	Yes 10 9 8 7 6 5 4 3 2 1 No
9	Do you believe people are generally only out for themselves?
	Yes 10 9 8 7 6 5 4 3 2 1 No
10	Do you find it difficult to talk about your feelings?
	Yes 10 9 8 7 6 5 4 3 2 1 No
11	Do you find you focus on work/business and find there is little time for anything else?
	Yes 10 9 8 7 6 5 4 3 2 1 No
12	Is it important for you to receive recognition from others?
	Yes 10 9 8 7 6 5 4 3 2 1 No
Total your score	

The higher your score the more likely it is that you are a type a personality.

Without adjustment, you are more prone to stress-related illnesses.

Above 85 points
Make changes

70 - 84 points
It will serve you, and those around you, to pay attention to the warning signs you may already be receiving.

50 - 69 points
Relaxed is one word that may describe you and you may still trend towards a higher score. Paying attention will serve you and your health.

Below 50 points
You are a true type B and little bothers you. It may serve at times to accept slightly more pressure.

> *What has your score taught you? This is another good point within this book for you to start thinking about your own personal style and how it is affecting you and those around you.*

Personal Perception - Strength or Weakness

We are one big habit and the definition of habit that I work with is:

'A habit is a behaviour that occurs automatically and unconsciously through repetition and over time.'

All our behaviours are habits, and when we want to change something, we must consciously think about the change until it becomes a new habit.

Without a doubt it takes more time to do 'things' in a new way and doing things in a new way can be uncomfortable.

What is your perception of your behaviours? How do you feel about the result you have received from the questionnaire?

If you scored high on the self-assessment questionnaire, please think about why you adopt that set of behaviours.

The opposite is true as well, if you scored low on the questionnaire please think about why you adopt that set of behaviours.

Neither is wrong nor right which is the good thing. Whether you are type A or type B naturally you can still get to the same result, just by a different route.

Both types A and B can get to the same result it is all about how you get there, and both A and B types can both experience stress, just for different reasons and with different symptoms.

The reality, though, is that type A tendency will be more likely to lead to a stressful situation or health situation either physically or mentally or both.

Our perception will lead us to our behaviours and our perception is, how we regard, understand, and interpret what we, and others, do.

> *I have changed my behaviours over the years, from a heavy type A to a calmer type B. Now don't get me wrong I am naturally type-A (I like type A) and I realise that I truly do not always get the best results utilising that approach and I already know from history that it affects my health and that of those I have managed.*

A true story. I had been working with an organisation over several years. The programs I had been delivering to the executive team were challenging and involved change to achieve different results.

A few of the senior management team had been in the organisation for many years and had become comfortable in their operational positions.

I received a phone call from the HR Department asking me if I could coach one of the female senior managers, who were experiencing difficulty within the new structure and ways of being.

Once again there were performance issues, and complaints had been received from the staff team and the customers.

The individual was a type B personality, very calm, very relaxed, very laidback.

The changes required had not been implemented, which ultimately had led to the individual putting themselves under so much pressure to, in some respects, cover up what had not been done.

They were too nice, did not want to upset anyone, did not know what to do and how to do it. The ultimate result and upset was far-ranging and far worse.

They had also perceived it to be a weakness to ask for additional support and help.

How you perceive situations will affect your results and the response that your body provides you.

We experience pressure from external forces. The perception we have of those pressures will affect how we respond to them.

Where Do the Pressures come From?

The main sources of pressure are:
1. Homelife
2. Work-life
3. Financial
4. Relationships

When the pressures come at us from every angle, there is little respite for us.

If the pressure is mounting in one area, and one area only, we can utilise the relaxation of the other areas to bring us back into a holistic relaxed state, thus managing the stress response and the toll it has on our body.

Stress – The Reality

Chapter 6 What Causes Our Perceptions?

Our perceptions as mentioned earlier, are accessed into our system via our senses.

The five key senses are:

1. Sight - I have a friend who when she sees a dog coming towards her will cross the road. We both grew up with dogs and were both bitten by our own dog. Her coping strategy is very different from mine – neither is right nor wrong.
2. Hearing - You are walking home in the dusk and you hear footsteps behind you. What is your reaction? Do you stop and let them pass, cross the road or run?
3. Touch - Somebody invades your space and puts their arm around you uninvited. How do you respond? Freeze and say nothing, repel them forcibly or manage the situation politely and request they don't do that again?
4. Taste – It is known that stress affects our taste and reduces the impact of sweet and sour items, which then creates cravings to have more to satiate the desire.
5. Smell – it is said that you can smell stress and a smell will trigger a memory, both good and bad. Perfume and aftershave can have good and bad reactions!

Now, of course, that would be so remarkably simple if it just ended there.

In reality, the information is taken in through our senses, it is filtered via our experiences, which provide us with our responses to the situation. Our coping mechanisms.

How are our Coping Mechanisms Created?

This is not the place to enter the nature-nurture discussion, let us work with, maybe, it is a bit of both for the sake of this proactive stress management tome.

All of our experiences in life from the day we are born to now, whenever you are accessing this information, at whatever age you are, are what create our coping abilities.

We are bombarded, daily, with so much information that we cannot possibly make conscious decisions all of the time about everything. Our coping mechanisms are buried deeply in our unconscious, as is the fight or flight response, and we access that information instinctively, in the moment, when we are feeling threatened.

How is that instinctive reaction created? Simply put we learn it.

The Iceberg

Imagine you are an iceberg - bear with me it will make sense.

What people see is only the tip of the iceberg and is described as our behaviour. Our behaviour is driven by our thoughts, feelings, attitudes, values, and beliefs.

Behaviour is a clear indication of what is going on underneath the surface. Dependent on what you read? It is said that only 10% of an iceberg is above the surface. By default, that means 90% is unseen and unknown.

That is the same as us, 90% of what drives us is unseen. My question to you is do you know what drives you?

> *'The skill to proactive stress management, in fact to life itself, is to become self-aware of what drives us and if we do not like the results that is achieving for us - change it.'*
>
> *Julie Hogbin*

Easier said than done I hear you say and that is the truth and it is all possible.

> '*Your experiences create your wisdom and you operate from and through your wisdom.*'
> Julie Hogbin

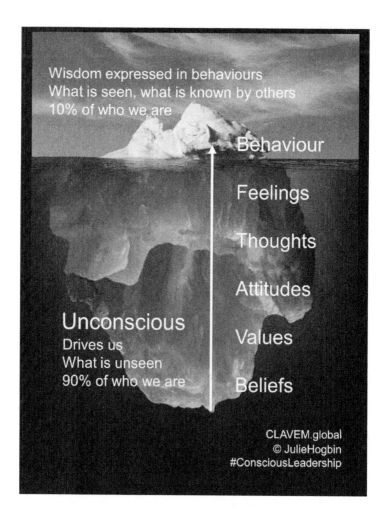

Wisdom

Wisdom is a virtue that is not innate, it can only be acquired through experience. You are interested in learning; you have accessed this information.

By reflecting on the learning and yourself, by analysing yourself and trying new ways and new things – you become wiser.

We start to build our coping strategies from the moment we are born. We are influenced from an early age.

'Knowing yourself is the beginning of all wisdom.'
Aristotle

'Have you 20 years' experience or one years' experience repeated 20 times?'
Julie Hogbin

Life Events that Create our Perception Filter

This list of life events creates and provides us with our experience and our perceptions, they teach us how to behave in the world, it is not exhaustive:

➢ Birth, pure and simple and decade, year of birth
➢ Parents, foster parents, adoption, care, the 'system,' siblings, aunts, uncles, grandparents
➢ Education – nursery through to University and beyond, personal development
➢ Teachers
➢ Faith
➢ Environment and culture – area and country of birth
➢ Accommodation – rental, private, low cost, high cost
➢ Financial recourse
➢ Peer group
➢ Work by its very nature
➢ Job, employed, self-employed, employer, employee
➢ Mentors, coaches, therapists
➢ Media including social media
➢ Pure experiences, pets, theme parks, trips and vacations

All our experiences are invaluable to creating the being we become and are, without any doubt. My question is the being you are achieving the best results for you and your wellbeing?

A Reality Check

Refer back to the Holmes-Rahe social readjustment scale points and the personality A or B self-assessment questionnaire, reflect on your result and responses and answer these questions.

Please think widely across your life.

1. What causes you pressure that you feel you cannot manage?
2. What do you perceive you cannot do anything about that 'stresses' you?
3. What situations create a feeling of unease within you?
4. What individual in your life 'upsets' you more than most?
5. What are you most annoyed at yourself about?
6. What situations have you come up with that you are concerned about?
7. What are you doing that you know, ultimately, is causing you harm?
8. What situation that has occurred in the previous 12 months would it serve you to get some help with?
9. What are you avoiding?
10. Who do you need to have 'that' conversation with?

These are 10 questions are for you to start a reflection process and identify one or two areas that it will serve you to address.

These questionnaires can be revisited at any time or frequency you wish to and please remember the Holmes-Rahe scale is a rolling 12 months.

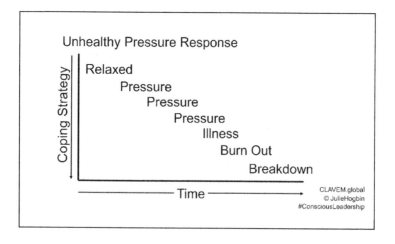

Please remember Pressure is good and Stress is bad. The ideal situation is that pressure is applied for a while and then released, allowing us to grow our coping strategies, and wisdom of what works for us.

A personal story

Life happens whether we want it to or not. I have once again managed to top up over 400 points on the Holmes-Rahe scale!

The key areas being I moved, My Mother died, (which was the 3rd close family death in 4 years she was preceded by my eldest Brother and my Father), my partner ended our relationship, I had new income-earning opportunities and a fabulous holiday.

There is more to the story and the thing is my coping strategies kicked in and I knew, to a degree, I was going down the rabbit hole. My thoughts were foggy, my alcohol intake went up, my sleep patterns were disturbed & I was grieving.

I, once again, did not seek medical help, even though a friend diagnosed me as depressed. I knew there were other remedies, and I sought emotional healing from an intuitive healer.

My system did not need to be shut down by pharmaceuticals, I needed to learn how to deal with my emotions.

I started the healing a year after Mums death and 3 months after that I was out of my brain fog.

Stress – The Reality

Chapter 7 Breaking the Habit

Our behaviours are our habits. When we want to change our reaction to a situation, we have to design a response that serves us and achieves a different result.

In reality, it is the same as we would do for any change that we desire.

Our behaviours turn from a reaction to a proactive response, we stop, we think, we reflect, we conclude, and we do something differently.

It is the age-old learning cycle. Initially, we may be in denial that it is us that has to do anything differently and one of the key things about managing our own stress is that we become personally responsible for our results and accept that we have a major part to play in the results that we are achieving.

> *'Our choice in any given situation creates our results! Our greatest strength is our ability to choose one thought over another.'*
> *Julie Hogbin*

Operating Reactively can:

➢ Allow you to feel bad about yourself. You see yourself as a victim of circumstance.

➢ Allow you to feel you are alone in this situation and it seems to be beyond your control.

➢ Result in you becoming stuck in a rut. You do not like the situation, but neither are you going to do anything about it.

➢ Be demoralising. You lose your will to work and adopt a defeatist attitude.

➢ Make you unpleasant to be around.

➢ You make excuses, place blame, and complain about your luck.

➢ Put you under pressure that results in stress.

Operating Proactively can:

➢ Allow you to create an alternate plan and choose your behaviour.

➢ Recognise that you have been operating in a reactive mode. You may not have realised it.

➢ Allow you to talk to others, ask for help, request their perspective and solution.

➢ Allow you to ask for the information you may need, from others.

➢ Give you a sense of control.

➢ Create a more positive feeling about yourself.

➢ Be a more relaxed individual to be around.

➢ Ultimately lead to a reduction in pressure and consequently experience less stress.

How do you make this happen? By wanting to change the outcome that you are currently achieving.

You implement and manage change for yourself.

A Change Equation

There are many theories around change, that I could share, and this as a change equation is a very good place to start.

It can be related personally very easily.

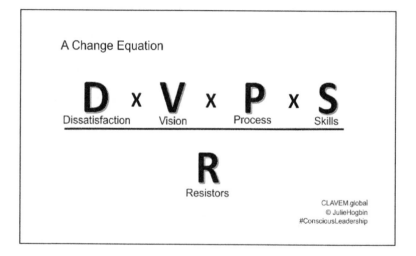

$$\frac{D \times V \times P \times S}{R}$$

A Change Equation

D — Dissatisfaction V — Vision P — Process S — Skills

R — Resistors

CLAVEM.global
© JulieHogbin
#ConsciousLeadership

D = Dissatisfaction

Dissatisfaction is the pain that you are currently experiencing with the overload of pressure. To change, the concept is that you become extraordinarily dissatisfied with the current status quo. This is your driver to do something different.

V = Vision
Vision is the future, vision is your end result, vision is the goal that you have in mind. The vision needs to be motivational and inspiring and draw you towards it, it has to be visible and inspiring to you.

P = Process
Process is how you get from where you are to where you want to be. The process is the steps that you will take, to make the change, manageable and achievable. This will include who will support you with the change.

S = Skills
Skills you may already have them and may have forgotten that you have them. Skills are your abilities to create the change that you desire.
You may also need to access the skills of somebody else or you may need to learn new skills.

R = Resistance
Resistance is everything that will get in the way and will stop you from doing the thing that you want to do. Which does include fear of change and the unknown.

A personal story:

In July 18 Mum died, I went on a trip for Business, followed by a holiday around China and Japan with a group of people and my partner. Whilst on the hoilday I was accused of having an affair on the business trip (I hadn't). The personal relationship ended, amongst some serious disagreements. I had a lot of pressure on me and was going through the process of grieving for Mum and my relationship - it was a horrendous time. I was still running my business and getting on with life, as I do, it is my pattern.

I knew I wasn't right; I made a couple of odd decisions (with hindsight) I was in overwhelm, and that black fog was close.

For the first time in my life, I really struggled, and I mean really struggled and saw no purpose with my life.

I had lost my identity, my Mum, my love, my future, my friend told me to take anti-depressants (now I know they work for some) but the thought of putting an alien pharmaceutical in my body was worse than the fog.

Now my friend is honest and for her to tell me that indicated to me I needed to do something, and I heard her.

I was dissatisfied with the place I found myself in.

I developed a very woolly vision - part of which was to smile again (that has brought tears to my eyes as I write *it) such a simple thing that was one step more than I had and please read and believe that I am one of the most upbeat positive people I know (normally)*

I had the D and a bit of a V, I also had some of the S. I know a lot and using that on me for me by me, wasn't working. I went looking for 'something, somebody' to help me.

I had received a healing session in South Africa in February of 2019, my first, from a good friend Debbie Taylor.

I think I went on an unconscious search for someone I could work with face to face and I found someone I resonated within August 2019, Kathryne Vere. I started the proper P process and after 3 months progressively getting better I found 'me' again (well ish) 'me' is still reappearing stronger by the day with emotional stability.

Now there were some R in the whole process, at times I was scared, like never before, and I trusted the person I was working with and went with whatever came up, that emotional 'stuff' can be challenging and it is what makes us who we are – ultimately.

The story doesn't end there of course, and it is far more than this, and I can assure you that if I can manage my stress so can you!

Being in Control

One of the first ways to break a personal habit is to become self-aware of it. With the information and questionnaires in the earlier chapters of this book and as you have been honest with yourself you will now be conscious of some of the things that you can do and change.

> You are now familiar with the early signs of stress and your sources of stress.

Create your list and then divide that list into the three areas, this will support you in identifying where you spend your time and energy.

The next stage is to identify those areas that you can control, those that you can influence, and those that you have no control over.

> NOTE: This relates to all areas of your life including how you earn your income.
>
> Just because we may perceive we cannot have the conversation or we have to accept what is happening – does not mean it is the truth!

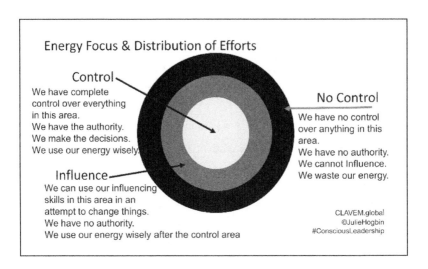

Energy Focus & Distribution of Efforts

Control
We have complete control over everything in this area.
We have the authority.
We make the decisions.
We use our energy wisely.

No Control
We have no control over anything in this area.
We have no authority.
We cannot Influence.
We waste our energy.

Influence
We can use our influencing skills in this area in an attempt to change things.
We have no authority.
We use our energy wisely after the control area

CLAVEM.global
©JulieHogbin
#ConsciousLeadership

Control – The 1st Area to Focus On

When You operate in the control zone you can make an immediate impact and difference to the results. You have complete control to make the decisions and execute the decisions without asking permission from anybody else.

This will be concerning your beliefs, your habits, your behaviours, your communications, your personal finances, your exercise, your diet, and how you show yourself to the world.

This will always be your first and primary area of focus to expend your energies into. This will give you easy wins, quick wins, and a sense of achievement.

When you focus on the controllable things first your power and energy and confidence increase. When you are operating in this area you become personally responsible.

You create your future, destiny, and results.

Influence – The 2nd Area to Focus On

When you have controlled what you can control you can then look at what you can influence with your newly found confidence.

When we are influencing things, we are requesting information, change, help, support from others.

How we behave when we attempt to influence others, to achieve something, we would like. Has a massive influence on the outcome.

Our approach needs to be planned, be coherent, and at times serve the person that we are making a request of as well as us.

We may ask for something and we may not necessarily receive, and that fear of a rejection or a no when we are dealing with stress, or excess pressure cannot stop us asking.

Negotiation techniques and a positive approach come in very handy when we are attempting to influence.

No Control

The no control area will never serve us to spend any time or energy in. We can do absolutely nothing to change anything that may fall into this area.

We cannot control the decisions made by the government; we can influence them with our vote. We cannot control the behaviours of others we can influence them with our feedback.

We cannot control what is printed in the press we can only control whether we read it and pay attention to it.

If we spend time and energy in the no control area, we are wasting it!

Very often people who end up operating in the no control area become known as negative, moaners, gossipers, and are quite frankly, at times, boring.

The 80/20 Principle

Why do I include the 80/20 principle in a book about proactive stress management? Because whether you realise it or not this principle affects your daily life in every aspect.

When you track back to the cause, the true cause, of the symptom you may be experiencing you will very probably find that it is arriving from 20% of your activities, 20% of the people around you, 20% of your diet, 20% of your work colleagues.

We live in a pattern of imbalance it may not be exactly 80/20 but it will be somewhere along those lines.

Use the resources at your disposal, that you can control, where they will have the greatest impact and value.

Rather than getting caught up with the trivial items, 80%, focus on the vital few, 20%, that when resolved will have the greatest impact.

Identify the areas where 20% of your effort will give you 80% of the returns, this will shift things dramatically all the better for you. Be selective rather than exhaustive in what you prioritise to work on to reduce the pressure or stress you may be experiencing.

Look for the area where you will get the quickest win with the greatest impact.

Being Bent out of Alignment

Let me ask you a simple question that has a deep response required for an answer.

Are you living and working to your highest self?

➢ Doing what you love?
➢ Working at something you love?
➢ Working where you love?
➢ Living where you love?
➢ Living with people you love – well at least like? (even if you are living on your own)
➢ Expressing yourself truly?
➢ In a loving relationship with self?
➢ In a loving relationship with another?
➢ Operating to your belief system?
➢ Living to your values?
➢ Being paid what you think you are worth?
➢ Being treated well by your line manager/board? (it applies to all levels)

Give yourself a score out of 10 and if the answer is not a 10/10 to any one of those questions, you are not living in alignment with your highest self?

The closer you get to 120 as a total the more in alignment you are operating and the more in control of your life you are, congratulations are well deserved.

My estimated score is 78 – there are areas for improvement and I am working on them.

I long ago gave up bowing to others whims, fancies, and power trips and not owning me as the person I am and am capable of being.

Now I had to learn how to do that and we all can. It gives us power back into our lives and choices are in our control. Even if we make a choice that would not be our ideal option – we own it and know why we are doing it.

We become a Victor rather than a Victim.

Speaking up and speaking out well and professionally, truly helps. By believing we are worth the best, which includes how others treat us, works wonders for our results, our stress, and our life.

Pressure applied to us by others is sometimes a good thing and sometimes not.

Poor management and a too heavy workload are two of the biggest causes of work placed stress within any work placed survey completed.

Now that does not mean we just become a 'yes' person and accept everything that is 'thrown' at us in work or life.

We are resilient as humans and being out of alignment for too long on too many fronts leaves us as a shadow of the person we can truly be. It will add additional pressure over time especially when we face more of what isn't truly creating happiness for us.

As women we have fundamentally, and relatively recently, altered our Neanderthal role, is it any wonder it is the female gender that experiences higher levels of stress?

We have shifted from a purpose of care and procreation, living in a cave and being provided for to:

► Care
► Procreation
► Homebuilding
► Education
► Work
► Financial literacy
► One parent families and
► Mixed families

Plus, so much more and how do we share the responsibilities? This applies to males as well; we have all changed our fundamental makeup.

We all have far more pressure on us than we are genetically designed to manage.

Two Ways to be Happier

1. Identify the times when you are happiest and expand them as much as possible.
2. Identify the times when you are least happy and reduce them as much as possible.

'We can intelligently change our exposure to events that make us either happy or unhappy.'

Julie Hogbin

Plus, an additional thought: Think how you can change your mind about some of the things you are unhappy about, think optimistically rather than pessimistically about the thing - there is always a possibility of a reframe and a realisation of a renewed passion.

'We are free to change how we think and act on any subject at any time.'

Julie Hogbin

Would you choose to make someone else unhappy? Your answer will be NO

So why do you allow yourself to be unhappy?

Whenever we hold back someone, somewhere misses out, and with Stress and the consequences attached, that person cannot be allowed to be you.

> *'Life is not a dress rehearsal, relearn to live and drive life rather than letting life drive and live you.'*
> *Julie Hogbin*

Operating from a state of appreciation and gratitude is not only the secret of fulfilment, but it is also part of the process of decreasing the pressures in life.

You have more vitality when you are grateful for all you are, do, and have. Every single day, stop and reflect. Think about what you could be grateful for.

Make it your aim to be appreciative of your life it will support creating and maintaining happiness.

A simple tip when you wake up, write at least one thing you are grateful for and smile. You can only hold one emotion at a time so start your day well.

> Create the masterpiece of your life one day at a time.

Stress – The Reality

Chapter 8 Culture and How it Impacts Us

Definition

When you look in a dictionary you will find:

'The customs, arts, social institutions, and achievements of a particular nation, people, or other social group.'

What does this mean for us and stress management? Culture is many-faceted and relates to any group we are in and to ourselves personally.

> *A common definition of culture is simply:*
> *The way we do things around here.*

What is Culture?

We usually think of culture in terms of nationalities, gender, age, religion, language, and governments, if we think of it at all.

However, every person, every family, every organisation, every team, every mastermind group develops its own culture also based on its:

- ► Customs - what we do, what we have always done, how we do it, what we have inherited consciously and unconsciously.
- ► Civilisation – our approaches, values, and beliefs.
- ► Achievements - the work itself, the success we have, awards, qualifications, acknowledgement.

Every individual is a product of cultural influences, we cannot not be. We are influenced by our environment, everything we see, do, hear, where and how we travel, what jobs we have and had, life and family experiences, etc. It's back to the iceberg much culture is created in that 90% unknown area.

Culture develops from the combination and interaction of each, and every, individual interaction we have with whoever we have it with repeatedly.

Second by second, minute by minute, culture is formed by what is done and not done, what is said and not said, which in turn affects the next interaction.

We all have choices, that is our human right and before we join a culture we do spend some time, often unconsciously, assessing and checking out the culture of the team, organisation, group family, relationship that we are considering joining and affiliating to.

Our Choices with Culture

As we start to 'suss out' the culture, one of three things will happen:
1. **Like**. We like the culture and fit straight in. We are comfortable with what is going on and we perform well.
2. **Challenge.** We are uncomfortable, not enough to leave and we believe we can change things for the better. We challenge the culture by challenging the people and how they behave. We take on 'the battle' we may fail miserably, or we may succeed over time. These actions will place our bodies in an aroused state as we may see 'things' as a threat.
3. **Leave.** We dislike the culture and we leave; this is where it starts to get interesting. We have two choices of leaving:
   3.1. We **physically** leave either the job, the team, the relationship or
   3.2. We **psychologically** leave but physically stay! This is the problem that creates presenteeism in organisations and life

stress in relationships. It erodes our self-esteem, self-worth, and value. This is a dangerous place to be and will put our bodies into arousal as we will perceive things to be a threat that we cannot escape from. This is truly insidious and damaging to our health.

Cultural Language

The language we use tells others a great deal about the culture we operate in both within a working environment and personally.

Consistently used such phrases can tell us a lot about our self and others.

The language we use is not just external, we talk to ourselves all the time, it is the little voice in our head.

Our internal chatter moves us forward and holds us back, it allows us to have conversations and stops us having the conversation that is required, if we are prone to negative internal chatter we need to change it, it will not serve us.

> 'Proactive Stress Management requires that we DO have the conversations, we MUST have the conversation with self and others if we are being negatively affected.'
>
> Julie Hogbin

What would you think if you heard the following?
- It will be a battle out there; we won't take any prisoners!
- Send in the reinforcements!
- Keep your heads down!
- Let's dig in!
- We're going for the big push!

These are very militaristic metaphors and give the impression of a hostile environment, characterised by conflict and the need for winners and losers. An atmosphere of competition rather than collaboration is likely as a result.

What about if you heard:
- I wouldn't do that if I were you.
- It's all a scam.
- They won't listen to anything we say.
- The last person that did that was ....
- That's not how it's done around here.

Negative and resistant to change language.

How about if you heard the following?
- What are your thoughts on how to move forward?
- Isn't it a fabulous day?
- Exactly right.
- I can certainly help you with that.
- I have generated three optional solutions.

It is a very different feel, positive, inclusive, acknowledging, and solution focussed.

Language can significantly influence how an individual or team perceive themselves and their colleagues and any relationship they are in.

Language heard every day is much more influential than a written mission statement which is rarely consulted.

> *'Proactive Stress Management requires that we DO have the conversations, we MUST have the conversation with self and others if we are being negatively affected.'*

This is such an important statement and learning point it is in the book more than once.

Communication is key with self and others to create a change.

List some of your most common thoughts about what you can do or not do. What is the voice in your head saying right now? Check if your thoughts are supporting you to proactively manage pressure or hindering you?

One of our greatest confusions isn't that we don't know what to do, it's knowing what to do and still not doing it.

Do you know that you need to do something else? If the answer is yes create, an action plan and obtain support to help you implement it - NOW while the thought is fresh.

Building Culture

If you wish to consciously change and build a different culture for yourself, your family, your organisation or business the following is a process to follow.

1. Identify the current culture, describe it as fully as possible in behaviour terms. Drag it from the unconscious to the conscious.
2. Identify the culture you wish to create. Describe it as fully as possible in behaviour terms. If it is for you individually you are in complete control, if it is for a group of people, gain their buy-in, and collaboration and influence well.
3. Make an action plan to get you from stage 1 to stage 2, building a new culture over a period to suit.

This will add additional pressure initially BUT for a longer-term gain, please add in relaxation time and celebration when changes are implemented.

List the first three areas that spring to your mind that you wish to change.

Chapter 9 Work Pressures

A Perspective

As mentioned in an earlier chapter we are pressured from various sources:
1. Work
2. Life
3. Financial
4. Relationships

For most of us, our financial situation and our relationship situation will be connected to work or life.

This chapter specifically is going to look at work which of course affects our life, our finances, and our relationships.

Much research indicates that much stress is caused through poor management and workload and of course that is not the only source BUT it is what we can go to the GP (UK) and get signed off work for.

That does not escape the unresolved pressure we receive from our home life and it sometimes puts us directly in the firing line of more pressure as we are then, off sick, at home in the midst of it.

Stress – The Reality

Many people I have spoken to over the years actually go to work to get away from the pressures at home.

Now, of course, that doesn't stop the pressures from mounting resulting in stress, which of course then affects how we perform. More of how we deal with the root cause in a later chapter.

Now for those in the entrepreneurial market, running their own business, you have complete control over your own poor management and workload! And of course, that adds pressure on to you.

It is those that are employed, in a job for a company, regardless of how large that company is, that are in a position where they, do not, have complete control over what they do, and when they do it.

Now, of course, I say that knowing that all of us regardless of who we are can change our positions, change our professions as many times as we desire.

And of course, we can change jobs, change companies, change professions, and change anything we wish to when we have the confidence, self-esteem, and self-worth to do that.

A personal story:
I was an almost straight A student who left the education system the 1st day I could without a qualification to my name (that's another story for another time) I left school on the Tuesday, I found a job on the Wednesday and started work on the Thursday.

I started as a shop assistant, moved into bookkeeping, moved into bought ledger, management accountancy, accountancy, auditing, financial systems implementation, financial training, graduate recruitment, graduate management training scheme, leadership and management training and all that entails, outplacement consultant and trainer, management consultant, leadership partner within a learning and development organisation, coach, trainer, mentor, consultant and property investor, public speaker, and author.

I have worked across four sectors: private, public, non-profit & entrepreneurial.

I have many qualifications linked to my professional capacities, I have been employed, self-employed, a business partner and business owner.

All from someone who walked away from an education system, has walked away from jobs, partners in business and life, and has been

> *stressed and used to hide behind her Mothers skirts!*
>
> *And who also learned to stand up for herself. If I can do this, you can as well regardless of what you think or feel right now – HONESTLY.*
>
> *Nothing is impossible – nothing.*

Poor Management

We cannot control how those above us, beside us, or beneath us in a hierarchical structure behave. It is firmly in that no control zone from an earlier chapter.

All we can control is our reaction/response to them and, if we choose to, attempt to influence them. The response option is always the better option of the two.

I have had many interesting conversations, over many years, with my own line managers who have been good and poor, mostly poor I must admit, and with my business partners and life partners.
It is certainly an interesting life we lead!

Over the years I have been a manager and a good one most of the time, even when dismissing an individual (another story for another time). My management skills were intuitive to start with, and of course I cannot do what I do and have done without learning from it and applying it to myself, I walk the talk and talk the walk. I always requested feedback on my performance, which helped massively for me to adjust the behaviours that needed adjusting.

As a manager, you want and need people to do what you ask them to do, you have to set a good example yourself. That doesn't mean you have to do the job and it doesn't mean you have to know the ins and outs of the job (that's another book).

What it means is that you become an individual that others respect and want to work with, they do not have to like you and with respect they very probably will.

Research indicates 95% of employees leave a Manager rather than the organisation! That is an incredible thought process when you dig into it.

> *'A manager's role is to create an environment where others want to be and will willingly do what is required – in a culture of mutual respect.'*
> *Julie Hogbin*

We can look at this for managers and what we also need to do is reflect that back on our self and look at if we are someone that others respect, it will have an impact on how we are treated both by others and by our self to our self.

Poor Management – What to Do

You may be one or you may have one and you may be in both positions.

When we receive or perceive poor management firstly, we need to think about why we think it is poor.

Identifying the actual 'thing' is key to how we can then actually deal with it. My true belief is that most managers do not set out to be poor or bad at what they do, they have their own pressures on them within the hierarchical structure and their manager may be poor in the skill set required as well.

Looking at this through a different set of eyes very often provides us with an alternate approach to that which we would normally use.

Many, many years ago I learned the lesson that if I had a problem and went to my manager with a problem it stayed a problem! By changing my approach to going to my manager with a solution, and sometimes even a few options, more often than not the problem was resolved, and on occasions, I got to choose the resolution.

One of the only ways to deal with 'poor' management is to arrange a conversation with the manager about the 'poor thing.'

Now we can only do that if we care enough about our self, the manager, and our working environment and are brave and have the courage, to take that approach.

> **Courage** *have a conversation with care, for them and you, using wisdom to put the message across enabling it to be heard.*
> *Cour – from the heart. Age – your wisdom.*

Often the manager is just doing what they have always done and do not know that is not conducive to being a good manager. Without being told they may just continue to do the same thing over and over as we all would – feedback is vital for us all.

Within most organisations, especially larger ones, there will be a process where this can be discussed and resolved. It is up to us as the individual we are to have those conversations and choose to do something about it.

Maybe your organisation provides a mediation or counselling service, has an EAP (Employee Assistance Programme) or Coaching and Mentoring, these may be provided either internally or externally and you may have a choice of individuals to work with.

A word of advice firstly ask and then apply to use whichever service is required from a position of strength. These services are there to support you and your colleagues and provide an element of 'psychological safety' and form part of the 'psychological contract' between you and your employer.

Within the earlier chapter on culture please remember we, of course, all have our choices on whether we accept, challenge, or leave.

What we need to do, as it will affect our view of our self, is to make those decisions consciously for ourselves with our belief system and reputation intact.

Poor management when accepted without challenge, can undermine our self-worth and our perception of our position, place, strength within life. It will affect our current skills and potential.

> *'Doing something sooner rather than later always wins out in the pressure and stress stakes.'*
> *Julie Hogbin*

Poor Colleague

You may be one or you may have one and you may be in both positions.

People talk about poor management very freely and very easily, and what I also see and discuss with people is the fact that the team members, colleagues, can be a cause of immense pressure as well.

Causes of Pressure in a Working Environment

The following list is not comprehensive and is a starting point to consider whether you are a manager or a colleague, a friend or partner.

➤ Letting people down, not doing what you said you would.
➤ Missing deadlines.

➢ Not planning, needing something yesterday or within a very short time frame.

➢ Imposing your values on others, rather than the agreed values of the team or organisation.

➢ Imposing your standards on others, which may be below or above that required.

➢ Being inconsistent, blowing hot and cold, some days happy, some days not, some days chatty, some days silent.

➢ Being aggressive, passive, or manipulative.

➢ Being loud and disruptive in a work arena that you share with others.

➢ Gossiping and being negative.

➢ Being resistant to change.

➢ Ignoring the feelings or needs of others.

➢ Changing the goalposts, frequently and negatively

➢ Talking over people, and not listening.

➢ Unclear roles, responsibilities, and authority levels.

➢ Sweeping things under the carpet.

➢ Poor communication.

➢ Not paying attention.

Please add any others you recognise and are not listed, this may be by you, your colleagues or your manager. There are spare pages at the rear of the book for your initial thoughts, please capture them.

Once the 'thing' or 'things' are clearly identified a conversation can be had, creating an understanding of the impact that behaviour is having with requests for change.

It will, ultimately, build relationships rather than hampering them. It will also improve self-esteem even if the result was not the one you wanted, at least you did something to affect change.

Workload

There are various things to consider with the workload as you may well have expected. When is one thing just one thing?

1. Do you have too much work? Or
2. Do you have not enough?
That is the first pair of questions to answer.

3. Do you have control of your work? Or
4. Does someone control it for you?
That is the second set of questions to answer.

5. Are you skilled in what you do?
6. Do you need training?
That is the third set of questions to answer.

Too much work is as much of a pressure maker as too little work and for different reasons.

> *'The concept of workload management is to get the best results, in a manageable and achievable amount of time, with people and the organisational vision in alliance.'*
>
> *Julie Hogbin*

It is not an easy challenge to get it right, and the only way to get it right is to manage it well and to provide feedback when things are awry.

In the times of doing 'more with less' 'lean working' 'agile teams' 'home working' 'matrix management' 'psychological safety' and any other buzzword that resonates, combined with cuts in budgets, funding changes and change in general, you can, when you think about it understand the issues.

So where does it go wrong?

It goes wrong when:

➤ People do not have the skills to do the 'thing' that is being requested.
➤ The team is not being evenly and fairly managed.
➤ People do less than they are being paid for.
➤ People do more than they are being paid for.
➤ Different standards and expectations are applied.
➤ There is simply too much to do.
➤ The manager says yes rather than no.
➤ There is a communication block within the organisation, messages do not get to the relevant person.
➤ People simply do not care.
➤ People delegate or do not delegate for the wrong reasons.

And probably most importantly.

The member of staff who is being asked to do too much, does not say NO and gets into overwhelm.

and

The business owner takes on too much, personally, and gets into overwhelm.

Both scenarios and situations are the same, ultimately both are self-inflicted!

Now I write that with compassion and knowledge that individuals feel they have more power in some situations more than in others, I get it I truly do.

AND

It serves us all to take personal responsibility and to do what we can, with where we are, and what we have, in the given moment.

> Giving our power away to someone due to a hierarchical position, in fact to anyone in any position, serves no one and no organisation.

Not managing our own well being and life and business just gets us into a 'bad' place and sometimes those that we love as well.

If the workload is too much do something about it sooner rather than later – it truly, truly supports everyone.

In fact, if anything is too much, do something about it, 'burying our head' 'sweeping things under the carpet' 'denying there is an issue' serves absolutely no one – especially our self.

Walking Towards the 'Thing'

We have many options and choices of how we handle situations.

Flight: We can of course physically leave the situation that is bothering us, which of course initially resolves the pressure. If the pressure is relieved and there is, absolutely, no emotional or physical hangover from leaving, then all is well.

Others may not know there is an issue.

When we leave on our terms, with our being intact all is well. When we leave, maybe feeling 'out of sorts' all is not well and there is a potential for our mental well being to be damaged.

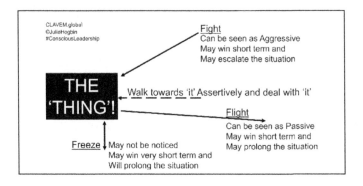

Fight: We can choose to challenge the situation with all guns blazing. This approach sometimes works and quickly, it provides us with a quick pressure release and gets the situation resolved, short term.

It may get the other person off our back or the piece of work redistributed to somebody else.

Others will know there is an issue.

As a long-term strategy and set of behaviours, it will not be effective.

Freeze: This is very possibly the worst set of behaviours to choose.

People will not know there is a problem, you remain in the situation with your needs unmet, the pressure increases, your health suffers, your relationship suffers, and ultimately your performance will decrease.

The most constructive option, which is not the naturally inherent option, is to walk towards the situation, have the conversation, and move forward.

This is an **assertive** set of behaviours that involves our interpersonal skills to be the best they can be.

➢ We have a constructive conversation.
➢ We deliver constructive feedback and praise.
➢ We accept constructive feedback and praise.

A process is discussed and agreed by both parties involved.

That does not mean that both parties always get what they both want, there may be a negotiation, arbitration or mediation process involved.

Whatever option you choose to take doing something is always better than doing nothing. Remember to keep the aim of making your life better and your self-esteem high.

Rights and Behaviours

When we are under too much pressure our behaviours will change and without responsive thoughts potentially our reactions come from the fight or flight process.

► Aggressive behaviour ignores the rights of others.
► Passive behaviour ignores our rights.
► Assertive behaviour balances the rights of others and our self.

Assertive behaviour will always achieve the best results long term. Assertive behaviour is controlled behaviour which will positively impact the situation and will reduce pressure.

We speak up for our needs in a way that others hear.

Chapter 10 Personal Life Stress

I cannot conclude this book without mentioning personal life stress and how we are personally under pressure outside of work.

How Do We Spend our Time?

Throughout the book, I am mentioning both and thought to write a list here specifically about where we can be under pressure and how we can put our self unnecessarily under pressure.

If you think about how many hours there are in a day, 24, we spend on average:

- 8 hours at work,
- 2 hours travelling,
- 8 hours sleeping which leaves
- 6 hours to do everything else cook, shop, wash, socialise, visit friends, family, children, partners and hobbies.

No wonder we are under pressure.

Plus of course the weekends. Now that is if we have a standard 9 – 5 type working environment.

Not many people I know do have a 'standard' type day and some folk are working 3 jobs, some out of lifestyle choice and some to make ends meet.

Let us take out work as that was discussed in the last chapter and the lessons that can be related to personal.

All those other areas add pressure to us.
➢ Travelling
➢ Family
➢ Personal relationships
➢ Friends
➢ Social activities
➢ Nutrients
➢ False friends
➢ Fitness
➢ Social media
➢ Financial

Travelling

It is extremely high on the pressure list. Whatever travel option you choose adds pressure to our life. If we travel by personal transport, we experience traffic jams, costs of maintenance, insurance, tax and the choice of vehicle to buy, four wheels or two.

If we travel by public transport, we experience crowds, delays, cancellations, the costs and very often must stand during the journey.

When we travel on holiday, we may choose to fly or ferry, which then adds the pressures of cost, waiting, delays, transfers, transits and queuing.

Family

Where do we start with family and the pressures that brings? In society today with everything as it is, we have blended families, and families living on opposite sides of the world.

Marriage and divorce, children, stepchildren, stepparents, grandparents and step-grandparents.

Family get-togethers especially around festive celebrations, christening's, deaths.

We are living longer which has an impact on health, hospital visits, finances.

Personal Relationships

My parents were married for 69 years I managed 4! They were in one relationship I have had 4 serious relationships.

Finding the right partner, if you want a partner, is an interesting process.

Keeping the right partner requires work, give and take, shared responsibilities, open communication, honesty and trust, among a few things to think about and possibly develop.

Leaving a relationship when we realise it is wrong takes courage, bravery, change and open communication, plus a few more characteristics as well.

Friends

Are your friends growing with you, away from you, do you have friends or do you have acquaintances?

Are your friends peer pressuring you to do things that you want to change or not do?

Friends in a working environment can be fleeting and if you are after promotion the boundaries of what you share and make public knowledge need to be considered in advance.

Social Activities

What are your social activities, are you the person that leaves work at 6:00 goes to the pub for a quick one and ends up on the last train home?

What clubs and hobbies do you partake in? are they high pressure or low pressure? are they expensive or great value?

Nutrients

I call it nutrients rather than diet as our intake should be nutritious, to fuel our body effectively and well.

With the advent of takeaways, fast food offers, and quick food because we are also busy, how are you fuelling your body?

Plenty of water, plenty of vegetables, and an appropriate amount of protein however you take that.

Less sugar, less salt, less carbohydrate, less cake, biscuit, chocolate, caffeine, processed foods. I am not a dietitian and I take note. I know how my body reacts with good food versus poor food and I know which one I prefer. Please relate this to the 80/20 rule it doesn't mean we can never eat any of these (unless we have major issues with them) it means we eat them sparingly if we need to.

If you are in a high-pressured stressed position it is vital to fuel the body well to rest and relax.

If our body is in fight and flight often it will store food as fat in preparedness to convert to energy. We are in the midst of an obesity crisis which of course affects health in general including our organs and joints.

Plus, if we turn to fast food and takeaways for convenience it affects our finances and if we eat late it will affect our sleep patterns.

False Friends

There are six things I classify as false friends, which individuals tend to turn to when under pressure. Why? because they provide a short-term fix for feeling relaxed. They ultimately and longer-term have the complete opposite effect.

- × Alcohol
- × Nicotine
- × Drugs both a) pharmaceutical & b) recreational
- × Sugar
- × Spending, gambling or shopping

All will affect our sleep patterns, increase our financial expenditure and potentially become an addiction.

Fitness

How fit are you? If we are under pressure with all of the hormonal changes happening one of the best ways to go from an aroused to a relaxed state is to exercise.

Dependent on how we exercise it will provide us with a social activity as well and potentially a new social group and of course it costs and takes time.

A walk in the park costs nothing and takes us back to nature.

Social Media & Media

The media however we use it adds pressure in various ways.

The media tends to focus on the negativity of life as it makes good headlines.

Social media, on the other hand, tends to make the world look very rosy and perfect.

When in reality and with an open pair of eyes we all know that the world is a complete mix, we have to edit and select carefully the information we take in and expose ourselves too.

Media can create social pressures that are, on occasions unhelpful as it can create a comparison state. Which can cause a negative perception of self if we judge ourselves to not meet up to the person, we are comparing ourselves to.

Financial

This is a big one. Money doesn't make you happy, but it certainly helps. We must have enough money to provide a roof over our heads, food on the table, and clothes on our back.

Anything over that is a bonus and of course, it is nice to have a holiday, a car, a social life. It is nice to attend and join masterminds and pay for personal development resources, it is nice to spend money on a nice meal out, it is nice to join a good gym, it is nice to buy nice clothes and live in a big house.

Julie Hogbin

When our finances are shaken it can have a massive effect on us and everything around us.

I have experienced redundancy and it was one of the best things that ever happened to me, one of my friends has experienced it and cannot see it as a good thing, even though it resulted in a better position for them.

We have different mindsets and coping strategies.

The one thing with redundancy is that you have no control over it, in most cases, so take advantage of anything that is offered by the organisation.

Coaching, outplacement services, counselling, talk to people and spend the time allowed to search for a new income stream whether that is a new job, a new career or a new way to earn money.

What is your financial situation, are you maxed out, living above your means, are you in debt and keeping up with the 'Jones's' are you living a materialistic life?

Please hear me when I say I am making no judgements; I lived that life for rather a long time and enjoyed every moment and then I learnt and made alternate choices.

If we are fortunate enough to currently live in a country that provides a government pension - is it future-proofed?

We are not all that fortunate, and even if currently you do have the likelihood of a pension, is it index linked and is it predicted to keep you to a standard you are happy with?

It is also nice to have savings and investments so that our future is secure rather than rely on a body that we cannot control.

Keywords Linked to Stress

Eustress. A positive form of pressure having a beneficial effect on health, motivation, performance, and emotional well-being.

Something we look forward to and none the less it adds to the pressure we experience.

Distress. A negative form of pressure causing anxiety, worry, sorrow, fear or pain. A negative threat is perceived or is realised.

Pressure. Is a force used against something to which there is a resistance. Pressure can be low or high and can be seen as positive or negative and it affects life and business. Our resistance levels will be different to the next persons.

Stress. A state of mental or emotional strain or tension resulting from adverse or very demanding circumstances, either saving a life or creating an insidious longer-term erosion of health both physical, mental and emotional.

Burnout. A state of emotional, physical, and mental exhaustion caused by excessive and prolonged stress. It occurs when you feel overwhelmed, emotionally drained, and unable to meet constant demands.

Stress – The Reality

Chapter 11 Top Tips for Solving Stress

We are unique and what works well for one person may be completely ineffective for another. What causes stress to one person may not to another. Our coping strategies are different therefore our solutions may be different.

We are wonderfully complex machines and the more we understand our own machine the more we will be able to help others with theirs.

50 Top Tips – there are more

1. Keep count of your 12-month Homes-Rahe rolling points, advance warning allows you to modify things and take extra care
2. Acknowledge where you currently are and identify what is required to do differently
3. Identify the major source of current pressure and design a plan to deal with it
4. Ease the pressure wherever you are able as quickly as is possible
5. If you know you have a stressful situation coming up create a plan for it
6. Find the level of pressure that is suitable for you, remember not enough is as bad as too much, find a healthy balance
7. Check the 80/20 concept, moderation rather than exclusion, when we deny ourselves of something, we want it more
8. Resist peer pressure

9. Do not compare yourselves to others we are all perfect in our own right
10. Establish your priorities for life or re-establish them
11. Recognise your accomplishments and praise yourself and if you can please tell others and if you can't learn how to
12. Focus on positives, we can only have one thought in our mind at any one time
13. Become aware of the inner voice, the voice in your head. How is it talking to you? When you hear it talking negatively say thank you and change it to positive
14. Control what you can and influence where you can, stay out of the no control zone
15. Source support, whatever that support may be and wherever it may be from, the more support you receive the quicker the issue will be resolved
16. If you work for an organisation see if they have an EAP (Employee Assistance Programme) that you can access, walk towards it and see it as a strength as that is exactly what it is
17. Be compassionate with yourself and with others, we are all in this together
18. Communicate, talk to people whoever they may be, your boss, your partner, your friend, your business partner, not all stress is self-imposed we are affected by others and they need to know and understand
19. Stress is not a secret, it is not a weakness, let people know you are under excess pressure

20. Laughter, physically laugh out loud, watch comedy that creates that laughter, talk to friends that create laughter within you. Laughter relaxes the body - you physically cannot be in fight or flight mode when laughing.
21. Training access the training, coaching, mentoring, therapy, intuitive healing that you need. To learn, what to do and how to do it
22. Use assertion, have the conversations that are required to be had, tell people how you are feeling, own your part to play in the issue, whatever it may be. Become personally responsible if you aren't already.
23. Mind control management, be optimistic, thoughtful, and forward-thinking, plan small steps to progress, whatever that means for you.
24. Meditate, meditation sometimes feels like a big thing and it can be for a minute or two slowly increasing in time, we all meditate when we go into our 'daydream' state and quiet reflection as a starting point will help
25. Diet, eat lightly and well and allow your digestive system to rest, eating late at night will impair your sleep. Cut out processed foods, reduce takeaways and fast food.
26. Establish what your body 'irritators' are and reduce or cut the intake of that thing – wheat, gluten, carbohydrate (I have discovered I have an allergy to Greens!)
27. Drink water, keep your body hydrated

28. Reduce false friends – caffeine, sugar, alcohol, tobacco, drugs both prescription and other
29. Reduce the foods that contain many of the irritants – coffee, chocolate, cake, biscuits, pastry
30. Eat healthily - vegetables and easily digestible foods, eat less meat (I love meat and have cut my portion size down)
31. Lifestyle - we are not machines, create a lifestyle that works for you and which includes nature, breathing fresh air, listen to the birdsong, admire the sky and marvel at cloud formations, smile at the sun and the rain
32. Have an orgasm - it relaxes the body and of course, we are naturally not in fight or flight mode
33. Rest and be still - turn the chatter off in your mind
34. Learn to relax - even if just sitting in the chair flexing and relaxing muscles and smiling
35. Put social time in your diary creating 'me' time and fun
36. Exercise - it allows your body to process the harmful toxins and relaxes the body - it can be as simple as a walk or training for a marathon
37. Massage - relaxes muscles tension and provides 'me' time
38. Sleep - relaxed sleep is far better for us than long or disturbed sleep, keep water by the bed and the room as dark as is possible it helps. Do not eat within a few hours of sleep it will disturb your sleep and relaxation

39. Help, ask for it for yourself
40. Learn to be on your own - with that comes peace rather than isolation
41. Create a culture that surrounds you with positivity, success and change, it will truly help
42. Break social media habits or at least manage them - pressures are imposed and not everything we see is as it is, it isn't all positive and beautiful and perfect, do not be fooled by it, learn to not compare yourself to others
43. Learn gratitude - it truly helps even if you write one thing you are grateful for every day - it creates a different thought process in our brain.
44. Keep things in perspective - remember what affects one person does not another so we can all learn from how others behave in similar scenarios
45. Respond rather than react - take time out to think about the best approach, practice and implement, remember the Einstein quote
46. Focus your energies in the best direction for you to get the result you desire. Remember where focus goes, energy flows and that is what grows.
47. Be assertive and if you do not know how to learn – it is a vital skill in life
48. Manage disagreement and tricky situations head-on, walk towards them openly, do not let them fester
49. Learn to say NO, politely and professionally

50. Check your finances and rationalise the spending, work out and change things to reduce utility bills, and CC debt. Get help if you need to. Financial difficulties compound to greater debt over time.

Plus one final reminder and this is the star:

Proactive Stress Management requires that we DO have the conversations, we MUST have the conversation if we are being negatively affected.

We must walk towards the 'thing' whatever the 'thing' is, it does not go away by ignoring it, and first we need to discover what the true 'thing' is.

Treat the Cause not the Symptom.

There are 50 top tips, there are more and this is as good a place to start as any with the basics.

Summary

I am trusting you can now see that pressure accrues from all angles, not just work as is commonly thought by many.

Will every one of us suffer from Stress NO of course we won't.

BUT and there is a but some of us will and please remember the costs to you and those around you.

Self-awareness helps us to manage our self and to create the changes required to stay healthy and happy. Learning to love our self is our aim and that leads to us respecting us which then leads to a healthier us and healthier relationships with others.

We acknowledge what is happening and how we can manage it proactively, regardless of the position we are in.

And if not for you the knowledge you have gained can help someone else. That someone else may be very close to you & experiencing the negative effects of stress?

It is key to remember that stress is caused by both positive and negative pressure.

There are a lot of people surrounding you who do not need to experience what they are experiencing, and I truly hope you are not one of them.

Please share this book, the information you have gained to support others.

I wish you all the absolute best and if you have any questions please ask.

Julie

connect@CLAVEM.global

About the Author

Julie Hogbin is a Management and Leadership Consultant, Coach, Mentor (and she knows the difference) Trainer, Speaker, Author, and a Property Investor based in the UK.

She has worked with 10s of thousands of Leaders at every level of Management and Leadership over 30+ years. The latter years working with CEOs, SMTs, Boards of Trustees & Entrepreneurs.

Julie has worked across with the public, the private, the non-profit and the entrepreneurial sectors. The Leadership messages are the same across the sectors, all are Business' where Conscious and Principled Leadership reaps rewards for all parties concerned as it does in life.

Her true belief is *that:*

> *"In the day of 'now,' those who think that the skills of 'yesteryear' will suffice will find out differently"*
> *Julie Hogbin*

and that there is a need to continuously develop to keep up in a fast-changing world or be left by the wayside. It has never been so important to change and adopt new ways of, not only working but thinking and behaving as well.

Crystal balls aside the more knowledge we have, the better equipped we are, to be fleet of foot and mind, and to change, the better our future will be.

Julie works with the human element of Business and Life and Julies passion is enabling others to be the best version of themselves they can be, challenging and supporting them to get to where they want or need to be.

Julie is ethical, honest and congruent, she walks the talk and talks the walk of what she teaches with energy and practical application.

Julie's first book The Life Changing Magic of Setting Goals is written to cover the psychological and practical aspect of achieving what we want from life.

She was also an authority author on Motivation in The Authorities – Powerful Wisdom from Leaders in the Field

Julie is a member of CiPD, IOD, CMI and is an Expert Accredited Coach/Mentor with the CPD Standards Office.

Please connect with me on all the normal social media platforms

Please connect on:
Linkedin Julie Hogbin
Facebook Page Julie Hogbin CLAVEM
Facebook Group Conscious Leadership CLAVEM
Instagram Julie Hogbin
Podcast Conscious Leadership on all platforms
YouTube Conscious Leadership

COACH PROVIDER: CE33010

www.coachofexcellence.com

Notes Pages

Julie Hogbin

Stress – The Reality

Printed in Great Britain
by Amazon